T0040382

the Readiness

ALAN GILLIS

the

READINESS

WAKE FOREST UNIVERSITY PRESS

First North American edition
Copyright © 2020 by Alan Gillis
All rights reserved. No part of this book
may be reproduced in any form without prior
permission in writing from the publishers.
For permission, write to
Wake Forest University Press
Post Office Box 7333
Winston-Salem, NC 27109
wfupress.wfu.edu
wfupress@wfu.edu
ISBN 978-1-930630-94-9 (paperback)
LCCN 2020940849
Designed and typeset by Crisis
Publication of this book was generously
supported by the Boyle Family Fund.
Printed in Canada

FOR

CIARAN CARSON

(HAPPY TO MEET, SORRY TO PART)

the Readiness

THE READINESS

It could happen at sunset
on a sloping lawn.
In a yawning estate
it could happen at dawn.

In a queue for your therapist,
in the public baths,
on a road through the forest
it could happen in a flash.

Under a harvest moon,
in a lift, on the stairs,
in an encrypted chatroom:
it could happen anywhere.

So make sure you're up to speed
when, at sunset or dawn,
worms vex the seed,
crows shadow the corn.

BEFORE THE BUSTLE OF DAY

The creepy wrinkled crawly schlong of the earth-
worm squinches
through soil to ooze in dew, only to be pincered
in the beak of a crow,

lifted above the garden, the gable wall, into a sky
of porridge
with faint pools of blue, bewildered by the air—
as you inch, bleary head

from your bed, braced for that plunge into the cold
stir of day—
but then ow! the crow screws up, bites down and the worm
is snipped in two

falling back to soil, through which both sides wriggle
on their separate ways—
and you could swear one version of you slips
from your thin skin

as you step across the bedroom's hard bare
floor to squiggle
back into the feathered duvet's womb, curl in a ball
and vanish there.

It is morning, this your morning song, your dreams
gone, packed up
in a past yet to come. Draw the blinds, your estate
is having its lid lifted.

A hybrid car ohms past and hurts the air
less while your
neighbour slinks home from his blurred night-shift—
the whole scenario drifts

before you like a strange spin-off from yesterday.
The trees see it all
but speak in code not yet deciphered as you go
through the motions:

get set for the whigmaleeries of the ticking clock,
spilt milk, the mystery
of missing socks, the transport peeve, the hundred-tonne
weight of to-dos,

as if in a slow motion replay when, by the door
getting ready
to leave the house for school, the little one asks
'Will today be a good day?'

Sizing up the right shoes, left shoes, controversial issues,
medicinal doses,
runny noses, mirrored poses, wet nurses, hearses,
drivers full of curses,

kiss-and-tells, infidels, cancer cells, generosity
and calculation,
intercourse and violation, plutocracy,
the erotics of accountancy,

white lies, undone flies, cosmic eyes, modes of thought
as yet unmonetised
amid the other thousand and one elements in the mix
of the morning

you waver in your tracks for a moment and think
of all things
of that bend in the river, the green-tinged turf-and-silver
sheen of that water,

goose-tongue and snapdragon on the banks, the solitude
where you lay
back to decipher the signals of the trees thinking this
of all things

is good. Yet since quality takes a quantity of time
to emerge
and will betray the cause of the beholder; and since, to be
a Gump about it,

quality is as quality does—worms get as juiced
over a rotten
avocado two weeks slimed and fuzzed in the compost bin
as you might

over the pleasure-mush and pimpled skin of ripe
strawberries—
you waver at the doorway wondering, when we leave
the house

do we exit or enter? So, ready as you'll ever be
passing through
the doorway, the half of you still in the hall thinks
to whisper 'let's fake it'

casting your shadow as the trees pretend
they're silent,
while the half of you already outside answers
'today will be what we make of it.'

BLOSSOM DRIFT (22ND MAY 2017)

Out the window four or five girls,
six, seven or eight years old,
circle and chitter in some form
of dance or ritual in the garden.

Inside the kitchen table is draped
with bright hoodies, a rainbow
of pencils, bobbles, bangles,
crumbs, puddles of orange juice.

They are constantly on the cusp
of cartwheels, giggles, a wee strut.
Imagine fourteen thousand
of them squeezed into one hall.

If there is a holy war, let heaven
assemble a nation army of pink
deely bobbers and purple nail glitter,
butterfly face paint, marching to a play-

list of Beyonce, Rhianna, Ariana:
let each follow the steps, learn the moves
of the dance with a gleam in her face
and unclenched fists, free from fear.

See them greet the orphaned daughters
of landmines, drones: each asking
the other 'What's your favourite colour?'
and drawing simple pictures of home.

Hear them sing 'We found love' together
'in a hopeless place,' blossom swirling,
through a dusk that falls from Paradise to here,
over the steeples, domes of Manchester.

TO BE YOUNG AND IN LOVE
IN MIDDLE IRELAND

The girl from the satellite
town holds berries in the fast-stream
supermarket queue.
She carries her longing like a stream of song,
her melody
a body over the border
of what is solid and what flows.

The guys in the depression-hit
town are tripping in the fruit
aisle. Falling for her
berry lightness they slip out
from their outlines. One guy says
she takes the form of a dream
or the dream of a form.

On the page of the regional night
berries pulse
like the notes of a song
in the stream. The girl
who sheds the skin of her longing
escapes into more
longing.

In a dream on the margins
of town one of the guys
hears a girl sing, her voice
like violins,
a basket of ripe berries
floating into the night
on a stream.

Undressing, streaming
from their outlines
through the borders
of town wrapping around them
the scent of fresh berries,
the girl, the guy, in derelict
bedrooms hear lucent songs.

Fingers in dark berries,
ribbons of moonlight
flow, fall away, come along.
The girl dreams a form of dream
or forms a dream of form:
the song of the night
undressed as a stream in the morning.

THE RETURN

If you take a moment outdoors as the day
undays itself, you might spot that swift prowler,
that tuft-tailed razortooth, red-stealthed stealer:
the estate's stray fox in the darkblue dusk.

You might hear that thornball in the shadows:
the hedgehog below the hedgerow—
wee nimble-nosed needlepelt, prickleback—
its spiny shuffle through dead leaves.

As the pill-faced moon spills weird silver
on the flagstones outside your back door
where you pause amid mint, rosemary, creepers
in the grass, you might reflect on your own

kitchen window's pod of light, its dark-framed eye
and seek out that silence-breaker—
that yellow-nebbed nightwing: the black-
bird silhouetted in the groin of a branch

become skeletal, bone-wood and wire—
and take a moment to consider
if you would fly through the night's coal and ice,
slither through soil, scavenge, pilfer the grot

as you enter, embrace your bright
children, shake off the rancour and rot
of another day's dolour in the welcome
of your kitchen's artificial light, or not.

IN THE WOOD

The gate is open:
exploding green trees
strafe a blue-feathered sky
swished by the breeze

that licks your tingled
skin, tickles your ear,
sunlight fretting
the path like a guitar

song that's jingle-jangled,
horny and harmonised
with soft carpets
of violet-blue-eyed

wild hyacinth and moon-
white may as you pass by
lovers singing me oh my,
past family picnics,

children climbing pines,
chaffinches, to find
a clearing where
nobody can see

you strip and slip
your summer body
into the rippling
blue scintillant lake

to emerge from yecchy
tarnished dead black
water in the shivered dark
and silence, a spewed

wreck slitched in the moon-
sucked wood where few
leaves dreep like bats;
where nothing resounds

in the quivering trees
and bramble but the hollow
sound of a rasping
wind as you follow

your narrow path
circling around
and around where
no gate is to be found.

LAMENT FOR A LONG DAY
IN THE LONELY ESTATES

1

You go away and leave us
you leave us and you go away
out the wan door, down hedgy avenues.
Gooning gulls prey over sun-snogged rooftops.

Schoolgirls laugh like milk bottles.
Oh fuck me her hair no yeah no REALLY?
You try to catch the morning tempo
hoping you look real, waving at Mrs. Kerr,

stepping over her big slobbery dog's splatter,
the lickspittle slime trail of a brittle-shelled snail,
to enter the temple of Ahmed's cornershop.
The usual crack: give us this day our daily. . .

2

The sky buoys your mind like a cinema
as you follow her past the laburnum
and laundrette, her outline a peninsula
in a brilliant sea captured on film.

In blue waves of sunlight her face is
like a plaster cast resetting the bone,
like a text from a lost child igniting the phone.
Then she passes out of focus.

You go away and leave us
you leave us and you go away
as clouds gather: the screen's darkness,
empty theatre, after the matinee.

3

You have rows of aisles inside you.
You push a trolley, picking up cauliflowers,
detergent, a Beginner's Guide
to Lucid Dreaming, letting them fall

into the cart. But a security guard
follows you, cameras fix you in their gaze.
You load the trolley high, join the queue.
The checkout lady's eyelashes are lovely.

Your fingers drum. Then the guard turns his head
and you run, you run through the mall,
the carpark, estates, to the horizon,
its bring-it-on, smile-a-mile, photostatic sun.

4

Press your face against spiny cobwebs
spun across coarse bark, running your fingers
through the privet, into the hedge's dark
thrummed with vibrations from passing cars,

farting buses, tall nettles, phone signals,
bramble quivering like a bird's nest.
You go away and leave us
you leave us and you go away

with falling elm leaves, breeze-blown laburnum,
its musk and splay, pressed into wood-moss
crawling with engines, camellia buses,
insects writhing, the passing cars' convolvulus.

5

With head half-baked
you walk away
from the bustle and brick
to the riverbank.

Three magpies hover and each,
there are no two ways
about this, feeds
on the corpse of a rat.

Yet they are magnificent.
You feel the sway
of the river, a faint
hum within the fernbrake.

6

The tick. The gap. The tock. Tick. Slowly, talk
to your pillow so the night will not pluck you
by the stem like a dandelion globe
and blow apart your every seed and speck

across these rooms, streets, parks. These, too,
return to atoms that will itch like regrets
or goads to start again, as your changing
world flows through you, its edge

and radius. You are in time and time
drives a wedge within as you go away
and leave us, adrift through the blue
or fallen drunk in a privet hedge.

THE INTERIOR

There is a bed.
There is a bedside cabinet,
a clock. There are no adjectives.
Whiteness is painted on two walls,
on two walls there is wallpaper
with boats on waves.
There is a window, a window
sill. There are no curtains
but blinds. There is a desk, a desk
chair. There is nothing on the desk.
There is a wardrobe, whose door
is closed. There is nothing else.

If we draw the blinds, open the window,
let adjectives in, we can see
there is not much bedness about the bed,
not much you might call beddy-bye
with sheets a bleached who cares non-colour
as if ironed by an enormous angry iron.
The whiteness painted on two walls is off-
white the way a joke can be off
or a person. The window blinds snigger
like blades, cutting the anonymous room
from the anomalous moon-shaped streetlamp
floating on the black sea of night outside.

The boats on the wallpaper fall
or rise on wave lines that peak
at intervals. I went on a boat trip once
and it was awful, the sea a grey soup,
sky a freezing fog. One might guess
that if anything was written on
that desk it might be gibberish but we
shall refrain from prejudicial speculation.
A lifetime of work to own a house.
A lifetime of work to find a voice
then you end up diminished by its
drone when you try to rise

to the occasion. Keener readers
will have noted there is no floor,
no ceiling. I recall standing, feeling
I was sinking, outside a bedroom
window one freezing dawn, the sky a grey
formless soup, having paced the night
to nowhere in particular—to this
window—I suppose thinking if this is home
then I'm at sea, at sea. At intervals
from then to now I have set out to find
walls, a row of rooms, strange worlds
within the wardrobe, whose door is closed.

THE RESPONSE

On a day like today you might lift
your eyes to heaven, but better
to lower them, contemplate the yarrow,
the dog daisy, the angel flower,
woundwort, mother of thousands, wild pepper,
goose tongue, snake's grass—better to narrow
your focus upon the thousand-leaved clover.

In the wink of an eye all you know drifts
away but who benefits from sorrow?
The earth still compels you weave a lover's
light flow, although older, sadder:
'I will pick the smooth yarrow
that my lips may be warmer,
that my voice may be gladder.'

ON BLACKFORD HILL

A brisk afternoon, the nippy air
could frisk through your layers up here
on top of the hill where the old man sits
on a bench with binoculars
ogling the porous shelter of the sky.

Other benches perch lonely and offer
different vistas of the density
of Edinburgh, its gradual dispersal
into sprawl and space towards its edges'
wider greens, rock faced hills

eroding in the wind beneath an endless
dilation of drifting blue, reverie blue,
headspace blue. But the old man's
bench is best: nothing in front but a clean
leap off the summit into the view,

into the continuous sky's great lift
and diffusion. So I think what the hell
and plant myself down with a salutary nod.
He nods back, lifts up his binoculars
with a grin and says 'the birds.'

The usual chiffchaffs, sparrows, gulls.
He says it's nothing, he likes to look,
to take the air. A woman is exercising
her dog with a stick, raising it
so the dog leaps like a hairy salmon

snatching the air. The old man
hands me the binoculars, points at a birch.
'Blackbird,' he says. I see only branches,
wiry briar, then look up to see white
puffs mutate in the respiratory blue.

Close up, it's no more near. 'You've more
interest in angels,' he says. 'The heavens
aren't bad up here, no doubt.' He says
he was in construction. 'Up scaffolding
on spring mornings, that's what I miss.'

A small child chases a football
with a resolute wobble. She suddenly
stops, looks up, out, then bobbles on
in circles, hands clasping above her head
trying to grasp the wind, the sky.

'Aye it's grand to clear the cobwebs,'
I say, thinking you need to be indoors
a long time to savour this raw normal,

this pristine now, the thisness of the air.
'I used to sit here with my wife,' he says.

'She said you feel lighter here and she loved
the view,'—he gestures to the blue, milk
and menthol seeping through it—'now I like
to come up each time after visiting her
in Cairdean House. She's in care, you see.'

An airplane scrawls over the slopes
of Arthur's Seat on a dreamish glide
through bluffs now tinged with a rosé
blush, lemon bifters, clementine swabs
above Edinburgh's disorder of rooftops.

I bid him the best, and as I walk
into the empty space before me,
the here of the air, it shifts over there,
ghosting everywhere and nowhere,
layer upon layer of nothing distinct.

Now I see the blackbird, singing nothing.
I turn around but the old man is gone:
an empty bench, above it windblown
whits or specks over chimneys, spires,
the infirmary, the crematorium.

The city lights come on, wrapping the dark
in their cellophane light. A woman shouts
at her dog, or husband. On Blackford Hill's
slopes, ice and ozone, I breathe in the air
and because it is not human, breathe out.

SCAFFOLDING

I set to work, try to compose myself
but all is construction, the whang and scuff

of a worksite out my window: the pile driver's graunch,
the bulldozer's crunch, the concrete mixer's motor-grind;

and my mind collapses to a clunch of greybricked
rubble-mess, gravel-dust; the grey-gunged leaks

of mortar streams, hose streaks; while pork-bellied men
in high-viz hey! hardhats ho! clang in commotion

so if I open my window for air
I meet the fair smiling crack of a builder's arse

then settle back in my orthopaedic deskchair
to demolish, build, demolish, build, demolish, build this verse.

THE WAY TO A MAN'S HEART

The tin of corned beef had a key
you'd turn to peel away the tin,
curling off like skin in a horror film
from congealed cleads of creamed gluten,

gicky lard and tallow that clabbered
the pink shock of that blood-jellied slub
of coagulate mince marbled by glops
of fat and sinus which you'd slice to slabs

for sandwiches adding globs of brown sauce,
its glar of vinegar and treacled
molasses smeared over margarine
on bread pieces you'd wrap in the crinkle

of tinfoil, as if to protect the rest
of the lunch—pear and flask—from their stench,
and my Da would light up in the morning
as he left: 'Lovely! Now off to the trench!'

TOLLYMORE

I've been full of meaning to return
to that woodland park near forty
years past where I hid as my sister called
'come back, come back, no-one's angry.'

Young soldiers troop past in forest
camouflage and from the birches a man
takes mock aim, winks and grins.
The happy-sad chorus of an ice-cream van

calls from the distance to bored girls
on holiday who lurk under pines as I spy
on their curved necks, eyes like cracked nuts,
their snow-white goosebumped thighs.

I'm crouched in conifer shadow,
green-golden reeds, butterstreaks of light,
still in the moment though all sways
in motion. Now try as I might

there's no way of answering
my sister's call: in a flash the forty years
stream out to sea; no way to follow
the bored girls, bluebells behind their ears,

sauntering back to the ice-cream van's scream,
soldiers swarming; and I furrow,
nested in that bark-must and water-light
deep in the high ferns' rushed and slow flow.

WHERE THEY SWEEP DOWN

Upward we trekked, the unstable sky
     floating, for now, a blue and white tie-dye
          scarf around the bluff
     swollen hill-necks ahead
where the earth bursts fit to wed
     the sky, weighed down with Kendal Mint Cake
          and Irn-Bru, buzzed in the air's fresh wake;
over the stile, past rowan and holly,
          their darkgreen prickles, scarlet berries
     keeping evil at bay,
keeping the stone cold dead
     from rising; big Phil already out of puff,
          lagging behind saying enough is enough
by the crimson riverside, his cheeks tomato-red.

Onward we trudged in unsuitable foot-
     wear under the sun ripe as a grapefruit
          by the Bloody Bridge
     river where legend
has it children, women, men
     were hung and carved until shins, ears, livers,
          tongues, forearms, ankles dropped into the river
     and the river boiled red through the earth:

Big Phil now looking like he was giving birth,
      trudging sluggedly over
sedge grass, ling, bulging
        peat like a morgue for lubbery sheep
          found deep in spongy bog ground
where buried bones give the earth its spring.

'Away up the hill and find yer feelins,'
      someone said, digging their heels in,
        'yah scabby fuckster!'
    A line had been crossed,
someone making light of Big Phil's loss,
      his dead mother. We scowled and spat on bunts
        of heather and peat hag. Soon a weather front
      would turn bog moss to mire, slake and slutch;
        all the landmarks we used to clutch
      hold of would turn to fog;
soon surveillance drones
      would clear these guerilla grounds and outlaw
        zones; small phones would dictate where to draw
the line, how to read the map, make it home.

Big Phil breathes in, breathes out. A skift of rain
      has passed and the sky's vaunted once again
        by the sun. He sees
    the heather catch fire,

streams flute down slopes in a freshwater choir
        through green-caramel glens to the constant
                dour and gorgeous coast; he feels omniscient
        air cool his lungs, under the carousel
                of black-winged birds circling bog asphodel
        and wind-ruffled bog-rush;
he slides down the bend
        of the hill's wet breast, along the wayward arc
                of the earth, trekking on to where the dark
Mournes sweep down to a sea without shape, without end.

UP NEXT, THE HOURLY NEWS

Sometimes I tune in
for nothing but the pips
that pip at the turn
of the hour on the radio

when you're never
quite sure what will come
next, if the hour will turn
or pip-pip-pip in limbo

forever; and those pulsing
pips are like fresh air—
although you know
they are part of time's

flow without them
you would go
doolally: pip-pip-pip—
like an opening door

as time splits to show
the chinks in its chain.
So time breathes
and bends through its off-beats

and no matter how cursed
you can listen for the light
pips of vexed time
always asking what's next?

DIONYSUS IN BELFAST

Big Andy, Wee Eddie, Fat Bobby and Sandy
in a BMW teeming with Lynx,
Blue Stratos, Brut, Old Spice,
catch sight of a foreign-looking glipe

on the pavement. 'I look for The Limelight,'
he says, and Eddie says 'Boys I thinks
we got one,' the fluffy dice
above the dashboard chuckling yok-yok-yok.

So they drag him in and race
for the estate, all bonhomie and shit-talk
but Sandy's thinking twice:
something about that strange-eyed face.

'This is not The Limelight,'
says yer fella, and when Sandy says 'look
we can double-back, let him be,'
Wee Eddie's yelling the odds: 'Ye spooked-

out-pinko-Barbarella-yella poof!'
Then the stranger sets free
his own weird hoo-hoo-hoo
and it's like his hair has dyed itself bright

green and is shooting up like a tree
through the roof of the Beemer
floating through the night's sea
of wine, fluffy dice bulging like grapes

and Big Andy, queasier than on bonfire
night feels a tongue lick his skin,
tendrils bind his limbs, while Wee Eddie's
nose grows, and grows, to a moonwhite

two-foot beak and Fat Bobby reeks
of kippers and lets out a backseat squawk
like Flipper. All turned dolphin, piss-streaks
through the night, they scoot off, diving for Belfast Lough.

INFLORESCENCE

Even without their fibre optics and shrill beeps
the flowers looked abnormal. Chrysanthemums
loomed huge, gladioli towered like human sized
sex toys of the future, a monstrous polymorphous
hibiscus swamped by whorls of livid orchids
loured in the shape of a wide-belled trombone.

The intravenous feed snaked from my forearm
into something like a sound desk. Similar feeds
were networked from the same console into the stem
of each plant and when the white-coated woman
flicked a switch a webbed mesh of illuminous green
tendrils, calyxes, stamens glowed. My forearm hummed.

'Now sing something,' she said. I found it difficult
to get started but the flowers straightened,
ready for performance. I don't know from what occult
source it sprang but eventually an air beckoned
quietly: 'I was sick and tired of everything, when I called
you last night from Glasgow.' The technician frowned

but immediately the belladonna lit up neon hyper-
pink and played a plaintive yet buoyant melody

as if a synth, and soon 'soup-pah-pah, troop-pah-pah'
from the clematis and enormous madonna lily
rang out in harmony and begonias sang 'beams are gonna
blind me,' flickering red, purple, blue and loudly

I felt my corolla open, petals within unfurling light
when the nasturtiums and tulips rose above themselves
for 'I know its gonna mean so much to-oo-NIGHT'
and the console blew—leaving only darkness, silence,
an overripe stench. She said 'steady progress' with tight
lips and wheeled me back to the ward's dismal fluorescence.

THE MAGUS

Lead me, skulking, through the polyvinyl
whiff and fooster of High
Street shops, the tepid white wine swill
of another morning sky

until the fugazi colours, perturbing sheen
of one store's
video advert on an HD screen
opens some inner door

within my hangover's armageddon
and I enter a green meadow
with Charlize Theron.
Yea, though I walk through the valley of the shadow

of death, corrupt, weary and sore
I still seek gold, frankincense, myrrh, Dior.

FLAT WHITE AFTERNOON

Forget about

        it for you'll

                never win

never hit the jack-

        pot and move in

                to a solar-powered mansion

to exercise daily

        philanthropy

                and fantasticate in

diaphanous pleasures

        but must sink

                or swim

beneath mood-mutable

        skies and coconut

                milk clouds

in the shadow of high

        shops, low sales, bright

                fronts, strung crowds

of literally miraculous

        people in

                expensive skin

like bed sheets

        you'd wrap yourself in

                              which you now touch
lightly as you enter
                  this passing café
                              past a clutch
of mitching girls
                  with pierced noses
                              and Tintin
hairdos who look
                  at you as if to say
                              is it dial-a-dickhead
day in here?
                  or maybe that's aimed
                              at the guy eating flatbread
with five thousand
                  friends on his phone
                              who types with a grin
all is well
                  with the world
                              when all is not well
with the world—
                  the burden of debt
                              heavy as sin—
although who'd be-
                  grudge this incense
                              of crushed coffee in steam
these latex flowers

              under halogen lights
                          and who'd demean
that woman with
              her small child wiping
                          the small child's chin
delighting an on-
              looker at the next
                          table over who scoops
two shaking spoons
              of sugar into a steaming
                          cup then begins
to call her son
              Oh my lost Son
                          asking after her granddaughter
while the mitching girls
              swagger out the door
                          look one forgot her
phone—ah good
              someone caught her—
                          and who'd begrudge the yin
and yang of this
              lingering moment
                          coming or going
here, there or some-
              where else stuck
                          nowhere and flowing

in the mix like

        everyone you are

                blurring below ink-dim

skies as time passes

        by like steam vapours into

                the run-of-the-mill grey

coat you put on

        pausing, before leaving

                to meet this falling day

which as your granny

        might say is the only

                day you're in.

METROPOLIS

(FOR EAMONN HUGHES)

1

But somebody must be accountable
I said
like a daytime TV village constable

with a dimwit sticker stuck to his forehead.
Well good luck
finding him she quipped, her killer red

lips a neon ocean sunset as she shlupped
my sidewinder
and we drank sex drives, wallbangers, headfucks

in that Titanic-themed bar fuelled by Tinder
and frustration
where every empty glass fumed with accusation.

2

Morning opens its door and the night
escapes through it. I pack my hangover
in a messenger bag and enter the roulette

wheel of the day, the forfeitured
streets, office windows annexing the world
wide web, doorways like mean cashiers

scowling at troopers and trudgers who herd
these pavements with microwave stares, debt
ticking in their chests, suspecting an absurd

hex was cast upon them while they slept.
As the city spins, by an empty chapel
a billboard asks how you like them apples?

3

I phoned. I tried again. She'd not pick up.
Emails, Facebook, tweets and texts all diddly-squat.
I tried her friends, I tried her work, with dodo luck.

I tried The Crown, I tried The Bot,
I paced the streets. No toodle-oo. No kiss goodnight.
Now in a reechy dull room I slump

by this whisky-tinctured window, a bright
red eye above the big smoke's canopy,
my cigarette burning, watching car-lights

disappear around the curve of the city's
surrounding hills, their darkness and whin,
like questions to an offline search engine.

4

Her mother said 'we've lost her. To the deep feckin web
I think they call
it—as if swallowed whole, always with her neb

in a screen. I'd be like, here love, you wouldn't haul
down to Tesco
and fetch the messages? And she's like sprawled

on the sofa with her head in her Lenovo
sayin she's quit
this meat space. I said sprechen sie lingo?

I'm only after beans and frozen chips!
Some bloody interzone,
who knows who's flashin you know what on their phones.'

5

I hoped for an on-the-cheap backstreet upgrade
but the man said no, the memory that matters
isn't storage, you've more than you need,

the memory that holds the present
tense together is where you're banjaxed.
Plus your processor's knackered.

Dismal, the sky a giant used Durex,
I walked this motherboard of high buildings,
streets and alleys, their haywired syntax,

generations of souls, living and dying,
failing and trying, with no way to process,
spun on the roulette of random access.

6

I finally traced her to an encrypted
chatroom.
All that she was was flashing text. She typed I've been lifted

to a higher form of self. It's like a door has opened
inside me.
I typed WTF? She typed you're not ready to come

through. I typed WTF? She typed take a tree.
Ok you can sniff it,
bang your head, crash your crappy Mitsubishi

into it but the higher reality. . . . She typed more shit,
finishing: I'm not here—
but did you ever stop to think that you're not there?

7

A lamp to relieve each soul of its burden,
a million interwoven—a pulsing glow
against the void's gulf, the stars of heaven—

the city glimmers: an electric flower,
a ballroom of desire, voltage and light
mirror-balled against the night's gloss black piano

which plays on you, pulls you into opiate
yellows, secret coral, retail beacons,
cats' eyes, green pills, fizzled pink sherbet,

bordello-blue harbour lights that beckon
to the boudoir of the sea, its oil-slick PVC,
whispering come to me, come to me.

8

Trees whisper you're not there. I put on the match and I swear
Gary Lineker
reaches through the screen to say I'm not here.

Sometimes my head feels like early Metallica
playing For Whom the Bell
Tolls, or like a featureless life-sized replica

of a cell: walls and windows barred with steel.
I hear her whisper
'unlock your mind and all that is solid

will melt into air—no walls, no ceiling, no bars,
no floor,'
as I bang, bang, bang my head off a locked door.

9

We're all born free, and everywhere we're in chains
that bind
tragedy to the goat, the hangover to the grain,

mazed souls to the city, damaged streets to a mind,
to a body,
to a door, each dog to the next dog's wagging behind,

her smile to the crazed dawn, memories to money
(though hopefully that one's wrong),
the dance in your pants that sets you free to Persephone,

Judas to the singer, Jesus to the song,
insight to doubt.
Now how do I open this door and get out?

10

I went down, bent like a question mark, each paved stone
exactly as mapped on my phone as routine
crowds inched and pinched the streets, looking for someone

to blame: pinging balls in a pinball machine.
Then a stranger smiled. The narked sky blushed,
babble chimed with bustle and I saw nectarine

untouchable light, light upon body-sized
vulnerable forms, filled with possibilities
and suddenly it felt as if the ground might rise,

the sky swirl down, the surface of the city
open its door, an answer mouthed in one soft kiss:
like this.

INDEPENDENCE

With such a way to
    fall from leaf to turf
the chestnut swells
    to burst from itself,

wrapped snug
    in its bright green
spiny burr, bristling
    to crack open,

rip away from
    its withering mothers'
catkins of gleet
    and dead flowers,

to feel the air's brace,
    licks of sunlight,
a smatch of earth
    before it's too late

high in the hold
    of interweaved
branches bobbed by
    winds, crisp leaves

in airborne spirals,
  rustled into scarlet-
yellow-flamed-
  umber seas of russet

where sparrows
  perch to climb
into husk-sweet
  skies—and it is time

to unsnig, let it
  go, cut loose and fall . . .
to be conkered, roasted,
  road smush, pigs' swill:

to be flesh to fruit
  the earth and root there
through five hundred rings
  to branch-tips from where

with such a way to
  fall from leaf to turf
the chestnut swells
  to burst from itself.

THE DOTE

When you laugh—I mean, when you burst
yourself open, gab and guts
in a quake, and the laughter becomes tidal
until you're well-nigh gurning with glee—
I'd dive into your throat to be flung
back out of your gob, out through the air,
recast and reborn, launched on your laughter's
hippity-tippety mad musical notes.

When you cry—I mean, when you deflate,
when your eyes play their sad flute,
I'd perch in your lug like some cartoon
doodlebug and whisper sweet nothings—to guide
you from darkened wood to garden
where you could take cover from this hard-
heided rain that will sift to dew
on the dawn's green-again lawngrass for you.

When the time comes to give your braw lover
yourself in a deep kiss under the elms
I'll lie in peace beneath a sycamore.
But know how, years ago, it was the quake

of your wee body, the voltage of your young
here-I-am—as the sun dropped from the air
onto elms, sycamores, harvest fields—that hung
my mind in the air, and left it there.

CYPHERS

After all, we are but pounds of meat.
We're lifted from our ground
by the swallows' flight over fields of lint

but can no more hold this than sound
or light, or air.
Like clock faces, we do our rounds.

We cannot decipher what shivered conifers
in the dusk whisper
to country roads. We invented reservoirs,

not water; we built storied tower-
blocks, not the starry-eyed
burst Elysium of their window-glimmer.

Yet each time I walk through these green fields'
moving shadows, eyebright
and marigold, I am looking for *the field*,

you know the one, dripped in honeyed light.
It's hard to accept
there's nothing more to the migratory flight

of geese as they cross the North Atlantic,
the sperm whale's
plunge and mournful tak-tak-tak,

the unfurling of the blue passionflower's petals
into a head-fruiting spawn,
or your own lover's radiance, than survival.

No-one is an island yet here we are confined
under the sky's
dream of blue, in the detention of our mind.

What we know is compromised
by the crime
of ourselves, the honey and pollen of paradise

all around us, each one of us a sign
to be shared,
each thread of connection, each line

a shoreline beneath a swoop of drifting birds
where the unknown breaks in waves like words.

LATE SPRING

Under cover
of the sycamore
wood anemone blooms.

The sycamore's
seeds, those nutsy
helicopters, twizzle-

twirl from cotton-
dabbed skies to crash
into yellow violet and vetch.

I remember
you were laughing at
a chaffinch, or some bird

on our tartan
blanket, all hoppity
risking its neck for crumbs.

We were naming
clouds, imagining
them boats on the ocean

before the bomb
of time disfigured
us beyond all

recognition.
I remember you
cradling some creeping thing,

the sycamore's
shade on your skin
like green-veined

white butterflies
and even now, picking
among the crumbs

left to us, I'd say
let no-one else feel
the under-foot dew

for you; even now
I'd say a green
world moves through

us in slow motion
among yellow violet,
vetch, wood anemone

under the ocean
under the eaves under
the chameleonic sycamore trees.

VESPERS

Everything changes.
In this there is no change.
The brutal day demeans
and the night sends its demons

not to overturn the scales,
so the captive are uncaged
and the wounded are healed,
but to remix and rearrange.

Only in the night
does the city uncover
itself in smudged light.
Above, below, beside one another,

dredged in a sea of dark wine
fermenting and fluid
we float through boundary lines,
ooze through the city's grid

of blurred walls, bleared edges, thin
partitions of metal and meat,
viscous shadows in a glow of molten
amber, berry red and blue livid streets,

decibels of silence and murmur
enfolding the present tense in deeper strata.
This is the city's distilling hour,
its night song. And the darkness is true.

She comes home, worked blue,
feeling like an undone bale
of dry straw. She drinks two
large glasses of zinfandel,

showers, does her face, steals
a few more, skirts spread on the divan,
and starts to feel how Emma Stone must feel
dancing in La La Land.

'Out of it.
I'm going to get out of it,'
he says, after another bullshit
day, 'right off my tits.'

In the bar they drink Becks,
Absolut and Red Bull full-tilt.
He says 'Jesus, look at her in her kecks.'
Getting up, getting down, getting into it.

The soft-eyed man at midnight
Mass kneels, his head at the hips
of the Priest. He cups his right
hand in his left and hopes

electric peace, tides
of mercy flow through his lips,
wine and bread become blood
and body, a slick and warm slide

down his throat, as fawn-
light in the transept blends
with the dark of night outside,
awaiting the scour of dawn

while the brazen lies of the day retreat
to do sets in a 24-hr gym,
toning their muscles harder through repeats,
making sure tomorrow they'll win.

After a Netflix
marathon,
rigatoni and Toblerone, she flicks
through her playlists, puts headphones on,

lies back
and sails into the wine-
flooded night, feeling music
trickle through her veins

blooming like a crocus:
her petal-like skin the melody,
her anther the chorus,
the rhythm and honey

of song resounding through the night
in the percussion of traffic,
the yammered and burbled flight
of voices, the ambience of electric

in the bones of buildings, the bells
of the streetlights' yellow
clanging through the night's deep well
to echo in solitary pillows.

The boy takes aim, puts one in the navel,
two in the head, and goes up a level
while a passing ambulance makes disco
lights in his high window.

Old-boned, liver-spotted, frail-aged,
darkness deep in their pillows,
they sink into their memories' montage
of first encounters, pianos

played at church hall dances,
corridors, weddings, new appliances
in narrow kitchens, their children
gleamed in backyards under the sun

that hangs like a cob
of buttered corn above the machine
of the city, smearing globs
in the windowsparkle, as dreams

mess with memories, and the syntax
of their final sentence on the shore-
line of sleep stretches to collapse:
exclamation marks become sycamores,

commas wriggle like snails,
hyphens turn into tongues
between the mouths of lovers, and cats' tails
slink like question marks among

kerbside bins filled with thousands, millions
of containers, mince grease, half-shlupped
yoghurt drinks, crushed biscuit, fish skin,
unspeakable tissues seeping to pulp.

While her pyjamaed partner snores,
sprawled across the bed,
she tosses and turns, her mind pours
and her body imbibes

absinthe shadows, the night's deep wine;
she prays for glistened
tongues, for dark-flowered vines
to twist through her limbs;

with hot palms between her
thighs she near-cries to the night: be ripe,
melt-lipped, river-creamed, let me rip,
devour for hour after hour after . . .

After pub hours, between the pub
and Kebabarama, they line
to piss, punch, snuffle through the flub
of their kebabs with an oink, a whine

while the soft-eyed man hits the pillow
like a stone,
his wife asleep, Gwyneth Paltrow
cookbooks by her side. He drifts alone,

glad she's found her way in self-management
courses and schemes of improvement
but wishing, one night, she'd undress
out of her newfangledness

to suede and swathe him in the rain
of her hair. Ships in the night,
sailors on wine-
dark waters. He feels himself float

above the window-eyes and cloudmuffed spires,
the all-angled architecture
of the city, outstretched above its wires
and microlights, weightless as a lure

over vents and funnels, trees of smoke
blown through the grape-ruined
air, the fennel wind; and he is poked,
bitten, nipped, licked, stripped, strewn

by the furies of the night, the bread
of his body scattered over gardens,
veins open to the wine-red
dark that kisses lipsticked lips and hard-ons

in alleyways, bent thighs in open parks,
arching spines in Subarus, public toilets;
and which kisses, also, the parched
lips of the unloved, night-pressed tulips,

pursed and pinched with the ire
of the fallen, the dropped, the broke,
the morphine-numbed, the sick in dire
cot beds, the butts of God's joke.

Engineers, warehouse stackers, students,
cleaners, doctors, labourers,
carers, dockers, guards, drivers, migrant
technicians, sex-workers

grin and bear it. In the brisk five
minutes they snatch from toil,
here and there, they filter their narratives
into ambient whorls

that buzz and hum in low frequencies
through the dream of the dark,
caught in the ear-cupped reveries
of those still awake—

perhaps yourself—sitting contemplative
by a window to float,
ebb and flow among these nightwaves
and scattering night-notes.

As if in a river of night-song
you drift past inner
estates, the suburbs' borders,
pulled by the verbs

of this dark river snaking
along waste grounds,
stony fields, past flaking
malls and run-down satellite towns

until you find its end—the mouth
of the night. There a babel
gathers under black wreathes
where you pause to mingle

on the banks with other cast-offs
brought here by the river,
carried by the night—strays and waifs,
your lost friends, first lovers,

characters from books long-since shelved,
women conjured in dreams,
outcasts, dead aunts, alternate selves
from pasts that might have been—

who gabble under the rowan,
witch-hazel and ash leaf
to watch the night's flotsam and jetsam
flush into the black gulf

beyond while they drink and blether
over the passing din
of regrets, shame, vexed desires;
and they usher you in—

'Is it yourself? . . . long time . . . long time'—
as you raise a toast
of the darkest, most head melting wine
to your own ghost,

dawn almost sparkling in the scales
of the snaking river,
the liquid night, curling its tail
around you to slither

and slide whole into your gaping
mouth. And you know this,
the oncoming day, is nothing
but the night's brief parenthesis.

acknowledgements

Grateful acknowledgement is made to the following publications in which early versions of some of these poems appeared: *The Café Review*; *The Caught Habits of Language: An Entertainment for W. S. Graham for Him Having Reached One Hundred*, edited by Rachael Boast, Andy Ching, and Nathan Hamilton (Donut Press); *The Dark Horse*; *Poetry*; *Poetry Ireland Review*; *Poetry Review*; *Poetry Wales*; and *Reimagining Irish Urban Cultures: in Honour of Eamonn Hughes*, edited by Stefanie Lehner and Sinéad Sturgeon (Cork University Press).

Many thanks to Don Paterson and to Picador; and to Jeff Holdridge, Amanda Keith, and Wake Forest University Press.

Deep thanks and much love to my friends, my folks, and most especially to Wendy, Vincent, and Rosie.

'Lament for a Long Day in the Lonely Estates': 'You go away and leave us / You leave us and you go away,' Jules Laforgue, 'Lament of Pianos Overheard in Well-off Neighbourhoods' (trans. Peter Dale).

'The Response': Yarrow song of last three lines found in Geoffrey Grigson, *The Englishman's Flora*.

'Metropolis' #8: 'All that is solid melts into air . . .' Friedrich Engels and Karl Marx, *The Communist Manifesto*.

'Metropolis' #9: 'Man is born free, but he is everywhere in chains,' Jean-Jacques Rousseau, *The Social Contract*.